Eileen Taylor

# Student-Athlete Mom

Your child was born to play sports!

Copyright © 2012 Eileen Taylor
All rights reserved.

ISBN: 0-6155-9809-9
ISBN-13: 9780615598093

# DEDICATION

This book is dedicated to my two children that are ten years apart in age...a boy and a girl...that participated in completely different sports. I am a blessed mom who learned so much about how to get college scholarship opportunities through their participation in sports.

# Contents

| | |
|---|---|
| Student-Athlete Mom | 1 |
| The Athletic Department | 9 |
| The Guidance Department | 63 |
| The Principal | 95 |
| Your Student-Athlete | 99 |
| Student-Athlete Marketing | 103 |
| Good Luck With That | 113 |

# Prologue

Most student-athletes have a mom that provides unconditional love and support. Unless the mom was a former student-athlete, she may not understand how to help her child manage high school with sports and get college scholarship opportunities.

The purpose of this book is to provide moms with very important information their student-athlete should know to get scholarship opportunities to participate in sports in college. This information is much more than just performing the sport in high school. Most importantly, this book is about reflecting upon being a mom and your child's biggest fan on the wonderful journey to a college education through the world of sports.

Thank you in advance for reading this book sooner than later and sharing what you learn with every mom you know. Sharing information empowers each of us to make a positive, meaningful difference in this world. Be empowered now!

# Student-Athlete Mom

**Unconditional Love at First Sight**

Do you remember when you first gazed into the sweet little face of your bundle of joy? I do. It was a bonding moment of love and personal commitment that I would do anything for my child. Nothing would separate me from exploring all possibilities to bring joy to my child every day of his life. This may sound crazy, but it's how I felt. I know that no one can ever know my child like me, because I am his mom. I took great pride in being a mom then and I still do today.

The next thing I knew, he had grown up a bit and was involved in the world of sports that I personally knew very little about. Fast forward to high school, and he was actually a very good *student-athlete*. Yes, I learned the word student-athlete when my son went to high school. That's when I became a *student-athlete mom* and didn't even know it! The strange thing is that no one ever addressed me with this title. However, this was a very important job of washing athletic clothes, feeding a bottomless stomach, carpools, cheering, and paying fees that I sometimes couldn't even afford. This was a job where I was in the shadow of my child and loved every minute of it, because I was exploring all possibilities to bring him joy...just like the first time I gazed into his sweet little face.

**A Purpose Written Book**

This is a book of *hope* for your student-athlete and you as a mom. This hope empowers you to *act* to help your student-athlete manage high school with sports and get college scholarship opportunities. As a student-athlete mom, I have always been amazed at how much information I learned on my own about managing high school with sports and getting college scholarship opportunities for my child. I was often frustrated that there didn't seem to be a single source *just for moms* to get information to help our children manage high school with sports and get college scholarship opportunities. It always felt like I picked up bits and pieces of information along the way. I began to envision what the world would be like to have a single source that I could go to that would *relate* to me as a *student-athlete mom* and provide information to help me help my child. This was the inspiration for me to write this book and develop the Internet website www.studentathletemom.com as a resource for moms.

This book is written *just for moms*. Although I welcome anyone to read it to gain very important information to help student-athletes manage high school with sports and get college scholarship opportunities. I'm assuming your child is already participating in a sport at any level as a student-athlete or you wouldn't be reading this book. However, if I'm wrong and you're reading this book because you care about student-athletes, I offer my genuine thanks to you for making a positive, meaningful difference in a life. You may learn information in this single book that you may not receive in four years of a student-athlete's high school experience. If you learn just *one* thing that you didn't know or understand, I have accomplished my purpose in writing this book. Finally, the purpose of this book is also about reflecting upon being a mom (or someone that cares) and your child's biggest fan on the wonderful journey to a college education through the world of sports.

It is possible for your student-athlete to receive college scholarships. The scholarships may be athletic based on sports; it may be academic based on grades; or it may be both! You just need to know information that can help you understand high school with sports as it relates to getting college scholarship opportunities. I learned the information in this book at the same time I was trying to help my student-athlete. He was fortunate enough to receive over $40,000 in college scholarships, but that didn't cover the entire cost of his education. I often wonder how much more in college scholarships my student-athlete would have received if I had known a source that understood me as a mom and could have helped me help my child. That is why I want to share this information with you *sooner than later* so that you can also help your student-athlete get college scholarship opportunities.

In this book, you will first learn about the student-athlete mom and discover that it's you! Next you will learn what you should know about the athletic department in high school and how it provides both physical development and personal lessons for your student-athlete for life! Then this book will open your eyes to the guidance department in high school and how it is *extremely* important to getting college scholarship opportunities. You will want to read and even re-read this part of the book until the information rolls off the tip of your tongue! When you get to this section, you'll learn why the guidance department is one of the most important areas of college scholarship opportunities support for student-athletes in high school.

The book continues with providing information about the principal of the high school. Yes, the principal of the high school even has a role in helping your student-athlete get college scholarship opportunities! Next, it's important to learn the roles and responsibilities of your student-athlete beyond participating in sports. Your child can personally be very effective in ensuring they receive college scholarship opportunities.

The next section pulls together everything you learned about the athletic department, guidance department, principal, and your own student-athlete. All of this information will be the *ingredients* you need to help market your student-athlete to get college scholarship opportunities. This is another section that you will probably read and re-read until the information rolls off the tip of your tongue! You will learn about college recruiters and what your student-athlete already has to offer them to be considered for college scholarships. This of course is in part thanks to you for being such a loving and supportive mom that helps your student-athlete manage high school with sports. As a result, your student-athlete will be well prepared to take on this responsibility alone while in college. You will be so proud! You will relax in knowing that everything read in this book falls into place in helping your student-athlete get the best possible consideration for college scholarship opportunities.

The final section is what I fondly refer to as "Get luck with that!" It was my loving way of saying to my student-athlete children that they were at their *personal best* when trying to achieve a goal whether it be getting a better grade in a class, performing well on a quiz or test, or breaking a school record in their sport. This section is my way of encouraging each mom to believe you have been empowered through what you've learned in this book to help your student-athlete manage high school with sports and get college scholarship opportunities. It can happen mom! So let's go ahead and get started with the next section about how there're a lot of moms out there just like you in this wonderful world of sports.

### The Community of Student-Athlete Moms

You are more than *just a mom*! Over 7.6 million *high school* student-athletes participate in sports according to the National Federation of State High School Associations. This number does not include the millions of *grade school* student-athletes that participate in sports each year preparing to make their high school team one day. Just image each one of these student-athletes with a mom just like you. Now imagine over 7.6 million student-athlete moms in the world of high school sports each year. Do me a favor. The next time you go into a grocery store, mall, or even the movies, take a look around you. Think to yourself, "Hmmm, I wonder how many student-athlete moms are here?" If a survey were taken at that moment, I believe you'd be pleasantly surprised at how many student-athlete moms are there just like you!

It's kind of amazing to think you're part of a sports community that large, isn't it? Well you are and will learn in this book what most moms don't know about how to help their student-athletes manage high school with sports and get college scholarship opportunities. Even moms that were former student-athletes may not know a lot of information that is provided in this book. I took the time to carefully research information that I believe we don't ordinarily get from schools. Schools are responsible for servicing an entire student population in addition to our student-athletes. And that's the way it should be. However, this is exactly why and how a community of student-athlete moms working together to share information with one another can benefit high schools with successful student-athletes attending that get college scholarship opportunities. Remember that sharing information empowers each of us to make a positive, meaningful difference in this world. Be empowered now!

Begin by reading this book that will give you an opportunity after each chapter to develop a personal plan for the information you've just learned and take notes you feel you need to remember in that particular chapter. Next, let your family and friends know about the information you've learned in this book. Text, Tweet, Facebook, phone, fax, or even gift them a copy of this book so they can also quickly get this information. You see I didn't learn about the information in this book until Thanksgiving holiday of my student-athlete's senior year of high school when he had finished his final football season. We felt a sense of heaviness in our hearts when we realized that his athletic talents and all that he had learned might not be a gateway to college scholarships.

I confess that I am human and was even tempted to give up trying to help him. It was this act of desperation that resulted in my family providing me basic information that I needed to know about to get college scholarship opportunities for my child. I quickly realized that I needed to know so much more than what they gave me and had so little time before he graduated. However, I love them dearly today with all my heart for inspiring me to remember that I was a student-athlete mom that would explore all possibilities to bring him joy…just like the first time I gazed into his sweet little face. I no longer had the very important high school job of washing uniforms, feeding a bottomless stomach, carpooling, cheering, and paying fees that I sometimes couldn't even afford. However, I still had the opportunity to help my child. Not much had changed. With six short months to go to high school graduation, I did not waste any time frantically helping my student-athlete get college scholarship opportunities. He got accepted to a college and over $40,000 in scholarships!

Now let's take a break for a moment. I want this to sink deep into your heart. This is exactly what I do *not* want to happen to you or any other student-athlete mom. Please join me and student-athlete moms everywhere in sharing everything you learn in this book about how to help your student-athlete manage high school with sports and get college scholarship opportunities. We have everything to gain! Our little bundle of joy that is all grown up now will be one step further towards a college education through sports because of our unconditional love and support as a mom.

**Surround Yourself With Positive Student-Athlete Moms**

Let's keep the community of student-athlete mom's very positive. Sports are competitive by nature. Let's leave the competition out there in the sport. I urge each of you to refrain from negative student-athlete moms. It's unfortunate, but they're out there comparing their student-athlete against any other child that may be interested in the same sport or even the same position. This negative energy *cannot* possibly be the fuel necessary for a good outcome in life after sports. Set a good example that your child can follow in life beyond sports. So proceed with extreme caution. *Real student-athlete moms do not embrace or participate in negativity.* Your job is big enough being focused on your own student-athlete that you don't have the time to engage in any form of negative energy about someone else's student-athlete. Most importantly, it's just not personally or professionally appropriate.

Put your energies into surrounding yourself with positive student-athlete moms. They're out there too! It's fun to have a positive student-athlete mom to talk to during games. It's even more fun to have their entire family meet up with yours for breakfast, lunch, or dinner during home or away games. These opportunities are positive examples of relationship building for your student-athlete to experience throughout the journey of sports. When I think about the experience of being the biggest fan of my student-athlete, I have fond memories of other student-athlete moms and their families that were positive and wanted the very best for their own child as well as mine. It puts a smile on my face right now just thinking about it. That's what I want for you, fond memories that you will personally experience as a student-athlete mom. So let's keep it positive ladies!

## The Village

When student-athlete moms, principals, guidance departments, and athletic departments work together *interdependently*, it is possible for the over 7.6 million high school student-athletes to be accepted and enrolled into college and universities. Now ask yourself, what is your personal *mom* contribution to this possibility that may benefit your child?

## The Student-Athlete Mom is a Parent Partner

College coaches and recruiters do not have the resources or funding available to become familiar with *each* of the over 7.6 million student-athletes nationwide that participate in high school sports. This is one reason why many quality student-athletes may *not* be discovered. The information in this book is also designed to help you *market* your student-athlete for college scholarship opportunities directly to nationwide colleges and universities instead of *hoping* a college coach or recruiter comes to high school and discovers your child.

When the over 7.6 million student-athlete moms begin to market their student-athletes, college recruiters may discover *unknown* athletic/academic talent that could strengthen their sporting program and overall university. Student-athlete moms serve as parent partners when they help attract colleges and universities to their student-athlete's high school.

## Notes ♥ Personal Plan

Each chapter in this book provides unique information. For the love of your child, there is space provided at the end of each chapter to make notes of things you learned or need to remember to develop a personal plan with action at the end of this book. This should assist you in helping your student-athlete get college scholarship opportunities sooner than later.

## Notes ♥ Personal Plan

# The Athletic Department

**Appreciating the Athletic Department**

The athletic department creates the sports environment in which your child gains the physical development necessary to get college scholarship opportunities. It hires coaches, personal trainers, and administrative staff plus inspires a host of volunteers that are responsible for the entire athletic department. It seems impossible that any one individual can effectively manage or take credit for an entire athletic department. People behind the scenes often get overlooked for those who are highly visible. However, the reality is that everyone working together creates a wonderful sports environment for your student-athlete. Working together definitely works!

The athletic department builds relationships with other high schools and organizations to set competition schedules and host events. It also hires coaches and professional sporting officials. Plus it manages the athletic facility at the high school. Who else makes sure it's stays up to sports standards, clean, and presentable for everyone to enjoy? Would a college recruiter enjoy visiting a facility of anything less?

As a student-athlete mom, I use to only think about coaches in the athletic department. I'm sad to admit that I never really thought long about anyone else in the department. I also use to think the coaches were solely concerned about getting college scholarship opportunities for student-athletes. If that were true and they spent a lot of their time in this area, when would they have the time to actually *develop* the physical talents of student-athletes? I had to quickly adjust and accept that the entire athletic department plays a *very important* role for my student-athlete. I also had to accept that the coaches are the best people to develop athletic ability and talk to college recruiters about my child's talents. I had to let go of the belief that they were responsible for getting college scholarship opportunities for student-athletes. After releasing this undue burden I had placed on the athletic department and its coaches, I freed-up a lot of energy to discover ways that I could help my student-athlete manage high school with sports and get college scholarship opportunities. It actually turned out to be much more fun!

One of the ways I began was to ensure I had basic information about the athletic department. Student-athlete moms need to know who is leading and have contact information for each member of the athletic department. This includes the Administrative Assistant who may be able to help you when someone else is not available. Student-athlete moms also need to know all of the coaches in the sports that your student-athlete is participating and have their contact information. If a college recruiter is interested in your student-athlete, they will request contact information for your child's coaches. You'll learn more about this later in the chapter on Student-Athlete Marketing. But for now, it will feel really good to know that's one less thing you need to help your student-athlete research at the last minute to provide to a college recruiter in a timely manner. Coaches may work for the Athletic Director in the high school. However, you'd be surprised at how many Athletic Directors and their staffs attend sporting events and may know more than you think about your student-athlete to share with college recruiters.

Go ahead and take a moment to write down the important names and contact information for the Athletic Director and his or her staff and keep it updated.

## Athletic Director

_____ name

_____ phone

_____ email

## Assistant Athletic Director

_____ name

_____ phone

_____ email

## Administrative Assistant

_____ name

_____ phone

_____ email

Do you remember when your child was in grade school? There might have been a nurse who worked at the school that your child could visit if he or she became sick. High school is a little different. There may *not* be a nurse on staff; however, most athletic departments have a Personal Trainer for your student-athlete to visit for physical development and should there be a sports related question or injury. Make sure your student-athlete establishes and maintains a good relationship with the Personal Trainer who is an incredible resource for your child. They should visit the Personal Trainer as often as necessary for physical development and get very *general* advice about health. However, *never* replace the Personal Trainer with your student-athlete's actual doctor or physician that provides professional medical care for your child.

Go ahead and take a moment to write down the important name and contact information for the Personal Trainer. If your school has more than one, be sure to write down information for each of them and keep it updated.

**Personal Trainer**

_____ name

_____ phone

_____ email

**Personal Trainer**

_____ name

_____ phone

_____ email

## Why so many coaches?

I have no idea! However, it is possible for your student-athlete to have several coaches, especially if they participate in more than one sport. You will need to be sure you have contact information for each coach. Go ahead and take a moment to write down the important names and contact information for the coaches and keep it updated.

**Coach No. 1**

_____ sport

_____ name

_____ title

_____ phone

_____ email

## Coach No. 2

_____ sport

_____ name

_____ title

_____ phone

_____ email

**Coach No. 3**

_____ sport

_____ name

_____ title

_____ phone

_____ email

**Coach No. 4**

_____ sport

_____ name

_____ title

_____ phone

_____ email

## Coach No. 5

_____ sport

_____ name

_____ title

_____ phone

_____ email

## Coach No. 6

_____ sport

_____ name

_____ title

_____ phone

_____ email

**College Recruiters**

One way college recruiters communicate their interest in your student-athlete is through talking with coaches and other members of the athletic department in the high school. There are discussions about your child's physical abilities with talent in sports and contributions made to the team. These discussions may be the inspiration the recruiter needs for your student-athlete to get college scholarship opportunities.

When the time is appropriate, the recruiter will want to personally discuss interest in your student-athlete attending their college or university. I believe this is where the physical abilities with talent in sports conversations *end* and the personal development achievement conversations *begin*. At this point, the recruiter already knows about the physical talents of your student-athlete. It's the physical talents that got the recruiter interested in the first place!

It's now time for your student-athlete to effectively communicate his or her personal development achievements and overall benefit that can be an asset to any college or university. The recruiter now gets a holistic view of your student-athlete as a person with sports ability with talent and personal achievements. Always keep in mind that over 7.6 million *high school* student-athletes participate in sports. With these numbers, you can be sure the recruiter is talking with more than just your student-athlete. How can your student-athlete communicate to the recruiter a high value to their college or university and receive a college scholarship offer? No one knows the exact answer to this question, but let's discuss ways to *inspire* the recruiter to *make* a college scholarship offer to your student-athlete. It can happen mom! We're leading up to much more about college recruiters later in this book, so keep on reading. In the meantime, let's stay focused on the athletic department.

What we've discussed up to this point are athletic department contributions to your student-athlete receiving college scholarship opportunities. However, rarely if at all, do we think about or discuss the personal development of *life skills* that is also provided by the athletic department. Even though it may not be thought about or even discussed, there are life skills that are *extremely* important to the development of your student-athlete. It's your job as a student-athlete mom to help your child understand that sports are more than just physical development. The personal development gained by participating in sports is *priceless* in life! These are life skills that are beneficial beyond sports. This chapter will continue by discussing 20 life skills that your student-athlete may develop in high school sports that have *nothing* to do with physical development typically associated with playing sports. Consider the life skills an added benefit to being a student-athlete. The upcoming section will describe each life skill and offer an opportunity for you to reflect upon your student-athlete's learning and development. You are then encouraged to discuss with your student-athlete how this life skill is a benefit in sports and beyond in life. This discussion internalizes what life skills your student-athlete has gained. It should also inspire a *credible* conversation with a college recruiter about how your student-athlete has gained personal development that compliments physical talents in sports. Most importantly, it demonstrates that your student-athlete is confident and can hold an *authentic*, meaningful conversation with an adult professional at the collegiate level.

When colleges are investing thousands of dollars in scholarships, it is a great benefit when they can enroll a student-athlete that can be marketed with both athletic talent and other personal attributes (20 life skills we will discuss) as an asset to their campus community. This may be what separates your student athlete with great athletic talent from another one of the over 7.6 million high school student-athletes that participate in high school sports. This may also be one of the ways your student-athlete receives college scholarship opportunities. When a college recruiter asks your student-athlete about strengths, weaknesses, or even a time when he or she was most challenged, the answer may be inspired by any of the 20 personal life skills that were developed through participating in high school sports. You never know what a college recruiter may ask your student-athlete. The point is that your student-athlete will be able to have a credible conversation with a college official that is authentic and meaningful. So are you ready? OK, let's get started with this activity!

## Life Skill 1 ♥ Accountability

**Description to think about how this skill relates to sports:**

- Accepts responsibility for successfully achieving what has been requested.

- Accepts responsibility for what has *not* been achieved.

- Evaluates what may *or* may not have happened.

- Celebrates achievements, learns from mistakes, and improves performance during the next opportunity.

**Reflection:**

- Think about a specific time that your child gained (or will gain) the opportunity to develop this skill by participating in sports supported by the athletic department.

- Take the time to journal it in writing on the next page.

- Make the time to discuss with your student-athlete the overall benefit of this skill in sports.

- Help your child understand how this skill will also be a benefit in life after sports.

- Go ahead, sit back and smile for helping your student-athlete manage high school with sports through understanding how much can be learned about this particular skill for life!

♥ ♥ ♥ ♥

## Life Skill 2 ♥ Adaptability

**Description to think about how this skill relates to sports:**

- Understands that *change* will always be a way of life.
- Adjusts behavior and remains flexible in response to change.
- Maintains composure during unexpected change.
- Accepts that change brings new opportunities in life.

**Reflection:**

- Think about a specific time that your child gained (or will gain) the opportunity to develop this skill by participating in sports supported by the athletic department.
- Take the time to journal it in writing on the next page.
- Make the time to discuss with your student-athlete the overall benefit of this skill in sports.
- Help your child understand how this skill will also be a benefit in life after sports.
- Go ahead, sit back and smile for helping your student-athlete manage high school with sports through understanding how much can be learned about this particular skill for life!

♥ ♥ ♥ ♥

## Life Skill 3 ♥ Conflict Management

**Description to think about how this skill relates to sports:**

- Knows that *conflict* will always occur in life.

- Accepts a personal role in the conflict.

- Adjusts behavior and maintains composure during conflict.

- Listens to and considers others' opinions or ideas.

- Seeks to resolve the conflict in a manner that benefits everyone.

- Accepts that conflict may bring new opportunities in life.

**Reflection:**

- Think about a specific time that your child gained (or will gain) the opportunity to develop this skill by participating in sports supported by the athletic department.

- Take the time to journal it in writing on the next page.

- Make the time to discuss with your student-athlete the overall benefit of this skill in sports.

- Help your child understand how this skill will also be a benefit in life after sports.

- Go ahead, sit back and smile for helping your student-athlete manage high school with sports through understanding how much can be learned about this particular skill for life!

♥ ♥ ♥ ♥

## Life Skill 4 ♥ Cooperation

**Description to think about how this skill relates to sports:**

- Respects different points of view.
- Accepts team goals.
- Participates in any opportunity to help develop shared team goals.
- Participates in team activities during and outside of competition.

**Reflection:**

- Think about a specific time that your child gained (or will gain) the opportunity to develop this skill by participating in sports supported by the athletic department.
- Take the time to journal it in writing on the next page.
- Make the time to discuss with your student-athlete the overall benefit of this skill in sports.
- Help your child understand how this skill will also be a benefit in life after sports.
- Go ahead, sit back and smile for helping your student-athlete manage high school with sports through understanding how much can be learned about this particular skill for life!

♥ ♥ ♥ ♥

## Life Skill 5 ♥ Credibility

**Description to think about how this skill relates to sports:**

- Believable because you have accomplished something in the past.

- Ensure you can do something *before* you tell someone you can do it.

- When you tell someone you can do something, meet expectations by carrying out the action.

**Reflection:**

- Think about a specific time that your child gained (or will gain) the opportunity to develop this skill by participating in sports supported by the athletic department.

- Take the time to journal it in writing on the next page.

- Make the time to discuss with your student-athlete the overall benefit of this skill in sports.

- Help your child understand how this skill will also be a benefit in life after sports.

- Go ahead, sit back and smile for helping your student-athlete manage high school with sports through understanding how much can be learned about this particular skill for life!

♥ ♥ ♥ ♥

## Life Skill 6 ♥ Decisiveness

**Description to think about how this skill relates to sports:**

- Takes action.

- Takes risks when needed.

- Makes difficult decisions when necessary.

**Reflection:**

- Think about a specific time that your child gained (or will gain) the opportunity to develop this skill by participating in sports supported by the athletic department.

- Take the time to journal it in writing on the next page.

- Make the time to discuss with your student-athlete the overall benefit of this skill in sports.

- Help your child understand how this skill will also be a benefit in life after sports.

- Go ahead, sit back and smile for helping your student-athlete manage high school with sports through understanding how much can be learned about this particular skill for life!

♥ ♥ ♥ ♥

### Life Skill 7 ♥ Dedication & Commitment

**Description to think about how this skill relates to sports:**

- Has courage to seek input for development.

- Has courage to accept constructive criticism.

- Maintains strength to work hard to be your *personal best*.

- Maintains endurance to continue working hard until you've achieved your *personal best*.

**Reflection:**

- Think about a specific time that your child gained (or will gain) the opportunity to develop this skill by participating in sports supported by the athletic department.

- Take the time to journal it in writing on the next page.

- Make the time to discuss with your student-athlete the overall benefit of this skill in sports.

- Help your child understand how this skill will also be a benefit in life after sports.

- Go ahead, sit back and smile for helping your student-athlete manage high school with sports through understanding how much can be learned about this particular skill for life!

♥ ♥ ♥ ♥

## Life Skill 8 ♥ Gathering Information

**Description to think about how this skill relates to sports:**

- A good listener.

- Has the courage to ask questions to gain an understanding.

- Ensures what is learned is accurate.

- Stores and re-reads if necessary prior to use.

**Reflection:**

- Think about a specific time that your child gained (or will gain) the opportunity to develop this skill by participating in sports supported by the athletic department.

- Take the time to journal it in writing on the next page.

- Make the time to discuss with your student-athlete the overall benefit of this skill in sports.

- Help your child understand how this skill will also be a benefit in life after sports.

- Go ahead, sit back and smile for helping your student-athlete manage high school with sports through understanding how much can be learned about this particular skill for life!

♥ ♥ ♥ ♥

## Life Skill 9 ♥ Honesty

**Description to think about how this skill relates to sports:**

- Has the courage to speak and act in a truthful manner.

**Reflection:**

- Think about a specific time that your child gained (or will gain) the opportunity to develop this skill by participating in sports supported by the athletic department.

- Take the time to journal it in writing on the next page.

- Make the time to discuss with your student-athlete the overall benefit of this skill in sports.

- Help your child understand how this skill will also be a benefit in life after sports.

- Go ahead, sit back and smile for helping your student-athlete manage high school with sports through understanding how much can be learned about this particular skill for life!

♥ ♥ ♥ ♥

## Life Skill 10 ♥ Influencing & Negotiating

**Description to think about how this skill relates to sports:**

- Develops and maintains self-confidence.

- Interacts well with others.

- Gains the trust of others.

- Gains the agreement of others.

**Reflection:**

- Think about a specific time that your child gained (or will gain) the opportunity to develop this skill by participating in sports supported by the athletic department.

- Take the time to journal it in writing on the next page.

- Make the time to discuss with your student-athlete the overall benefit of this skill in sports.

- Help your child understand how this skill will also be a benefit in life after sports.

- Go ahead, sit back and smile for helping your student-athlete manage high school with sports through understanding how much can be learned about this particular skill for life!

♥ ♥ ♥ ♥

## Life Skill 11 ♥ Integrity

**Description to think about how this skill relates to sports:**

- Acts with righteousness.

- Maintains positive behavior especially when tempted with negativity.

- Acts in a behavior consistent with values of family and high school.

- Keeps commitments and does not make commitments that cannot be kept.

- Accepts consequences for actions.

**Reflection:**

- Think about a specific time that your child gained (or will gain) the opportunity to develop this skill by participating in sports supported by the athletic department.

- Take the time to journal it in writing on the next page.

- Make the time to discuss with your student-athlete the overall benefit of this skill in sports.

- Help your child understand how this skill will also be a benefit in life after sports.

- Go ahead, sit back and smile for helping your student-athlete manage high school with sports through understanding how much can be learned about this particular skill for life!

♥ ♥ ♥ ♥

## Life Skill 12 ♥ Oral Communications

### Description to think about how this skill relates to sports:

- Develops and maintains self-confidence.

- Has the courage to ask questions to gain an understanding.

- Has the courage to express and respect differing opinions.

### Reflection:

- Think about a specific time that your child gained (or will gain) the opportunity to develop this skill by participating in sports supported by the athletic department.

- Take the time to journal it in writing on the next page.

- Make the time to discuss with your student-athlete the overall benefit of this skill in sports.

- Help your child understand how this skill will also be a benefit in life after sports.

- Go ahead, sit back and smile for helping your student-athlete manage high school with sports through understanding how much can be learned about this particular skill for life!

♥ ♥ ♥ ♥

## Life Skill 13 ♥ Planning & Organizing

**Description to think about how this skill relates to sports:**

- Takes the time to examine what needs to be done and prioritizes for successful outcomes.

- Makes the time to evaluate outcomes to determine if it is worthy of doing again.

**Reflection:**

- Think about a specific time that your child gained (or will gain) the opportunity to develop this skill by participating in sports supported by the athletic department.

- Take the time to journal it in writing on the next page.

- Make the time to discuss with your student-athlete the overall benefit of this skill in sports.

- Help your child understand how this skill will also be a benefit in life after sports.

- Go ahead, sit back and smile for helping your student-athlete manage high school with sports through understanding how much can be learned about this particular skill for life!

♥ ♥ ♥ ♥

## Life Skill 14 ♥ Problem Solving

### Description to think about how this skill relates to sports:

- Knows that *problems* will always occur in life.

- Adjusts behavior and remains flexible in response to problem solving.

- Maintains composure during problem solving.

- Has the courage to seek solutions to the problem.

- Has the courage to make a decision to solve a problem.

- Accepts the outcome of the decision.

- Accepts that problem solving brings new opportunities in life.

### Reflection:

- Think about a specific time that your child gained (or will gain) the opportunity to develop this skill by participating in sports supported by the athletic department.

- Take the time to journal it in writing on the next page.

- Make the time to discuss with your student-athlete the overall benefit of this skill in sports.

- Help your child understand how this skill will also be a benefit in life after sports.

- Go ahead, sit back and smile for helping your student-athlete manage high school with sports through understanding how much can be learned about this particular skill for life!

♥ ♥ ♥ ♥

## Life Skill 15 ♥ Professionalism

**Description to think about how this skill relates to sports:**

- Acts in a behavior consistent with family values.

- Acts in a behavior consistent with high school values.

- Maintains positive behavior especially when tempted with negativity.

**Reflection:**

- Think about a specific time that your child gained (or will gain) the opportunity to develop this skill by participating in sports supported by the athletic department.

- Take the time to journal it in writing on the next page.

- Make the time to discuss with your student-athlete the overall benefit of this skill in sports.

- Help your child understand how this skill will also be a benefit in life after sports.

- Go ahead, sit back and smile for helping your student-athlete manage high school with sports through understanding how much can be learned about this particular skill for life!

♥ ♥ ♥ ♥

## Life Skill 16 ♥ Self Management

**Description to think about how this skill relates to sports:**

- Knows personal strengths with a desire to maintain or improve.

- Knows personal challenges with a desire to improve.

- Aware of personal impact on others.

- Focuses on present requirements and commitments.

- Plans and prepares for future requirements and commitments.

**Reflection:**

- Think about a specific time that your child gained (or will gain) the opportunity to develop this skill by participating in sports supported by the athletic department.

- Take the time to journal it in writing on the next page.

- Make the time to discuss with your student-athlete the overall benefit of this skill in sports.

- Help your child understand how this skill will also be a benefit in life after sports.

- Go ahead, sit back and smile for helping your student-athlete manage high school with sports through understanding how much can be learned about this particular skill for life!

♥ ♥ ♥ ♥

## Life Skill 17 ♥ Teamwork

### Description to think about how this skill relates to sports:

- Understands that people are unique individuals with different talents and abilities.

- Understands that this uniqueness when respected and working together makes for an even better team.

- Inspires this even better team to be motivated to achieve their goals.

- Encourages the team to build trust with one another to eliminate barriers to achieving team goals.

### Reflection:

- Think about a specific time that your child gained (or will gain) the opportunity to develop this skill by participating in sports supported by the athletic department.

- Take the time to journal it in writing on the next page.

- Make the time to discuss with your student-athlete the overall benefit of this skill in sports.

- Help your child understand how this skill will also be a benefit in life after sports.

- Go ahead, sit back and smile for helping your student-athlete manage high school with sports through understanding how much can be learned about this particular skill for life!

♥ ♥ ♥ ♥

## Life Skill 18 ♥ Time Management

**Description to think about how this skill relates to sports:**

- Values own time.

- Respects the time of others.

- Maintains a calendar to keep track of activities and commitments.

- Keeps commitments.

- Arrives on time and stays throughout the activity or commitment.

- Does not make commitments that cannot be honored.

**Reflection:**

- Think about a specific time that your child gained (or will gain) the opportunity to develop this skill by participating in sports supported by the athletic department.

- Take the time to journal it in writing on the next page.

- Make the time to discuss with your student-athlete the overall benefit of this skill in sports.

- Help your child understand how this skill will also be a benefit in life after sports.

- Go ahead, sit back and smile for helping your student-athlete manage high school with sports through understanding how much can be learned about this particular skill for life!

♥ ♥ ♥ ♥

## Life Skill 19 ♥ Work Ethic

**Description to think about how this skill relates to sports:**

- Arrives on time and stays throughout the activity or commitment.

- Demonstrates dedication.

- Demonstrates loyalty.

- Motivated to work consistently.

- Perseveres.

**Reflection:**

- Think about a specific time that your child gained (or will gain) the opportunity to develop this skill by participating in sports supported by the athletic department.

- Take the time to journal it in writing on the next page.

- Make the time to discuss with your student-athlete the overall benefit of this skill in sports.

- Help your child understand how this skill will also be a benefit in life after sports.

- Go ahead, sit back and smile for helping your student-athlete manage high school with sports through understanding how much can be learned about this particular skill for life!

♥ ♥ ♥ ♥

## Life Skill 20 ♥ Written Communications

**Description to think about how this skill relates to sports:**

- Communicates effectively in response to requests for information.

- Provides information in a timely manner.

**Reflection:**

- Think about a specific time that your child gained (or will gain) the opportunity to develop this skill by participating in sports supported by the athletic department.

- Take the time to journal it in writing on the next page.

- Make the time to discuss with your student-athlete the overall benefit of this skill in sports.

- Help your child understand how this skill will also be a benefit in life after sports.

- Go ahead, sit back and smile for helping your student-athlete manage high school with sports through understanding how much can be learned about this particular skill for life!

♥ ♥ ♥ ♥

**Notes ♥ Personal Plan**

# The Guidance Department

**Great Little Known Information**

This is one of my favorite chapters, because it helped me understand why some of the very *best* physically talented athletes may *not* be participating in college sports. It gave me *hope* for my student-athlete that you can also have for your child. In this chapter you will learn facts that have everything to do with *academic* classes and grades for your student-athlete and *nothing* to do with participating in the actual sport. Yes, that's correct! You see, no matter how talented your student-athlete is in participating in a sport, there is a minimum *academic* requirement to be met to receive college scholarship opportunities in many cases. As a student-athlete mom, you will want to know about these academic requirements. Otherwise, you'll be like some student-athlete moms that believe their child's athletic ability will override poor academic performance. This is a setup for a BIG disappointment for the student-athlete and mom. I don't want to see this happen to you or your child.

I once knew a widely known and talented student-athlete that was unable to play for the high school due to less than acceptable academic performance. The student-athlete had become *ineligible* to participate in the sport due to grades. In all the times that we had heard about and seen this student-athlete perform, I would have never imagined there could be an academic challenge. This is because there was always a lot of hype about the actual sport performance and nothing about the academic performance. Don't be surprised, because this happens all the time. College recruiters first learn about student-athletes due to their sports performance, and later learn about their academic performance. This may result in college scholarship opportunities for other student-athletes that may not be as physically talented. So when you hear that a student-athlete is "ineligible" to participate in a sport, it may be directly related to academic performance as measured by grades.

This is why your child is referred to as a *student-athlete*. To be eligible to receive scholarships to participate in sports at many colleges and universities that offer a high competitive level, your student-athlete must have taken specific types of classes in high school, earned an acceptable grade point average (GPA), as well as earned an acceptable score on either the ACT or SAT college entrance exams. The good news is that most high schools are aware of this requirement and offer the specific type of classes as part of their normal academic schedules.

Most high schools also do *not* allow student-athletes to participate in sports with less than acceptable grades. So this puts the academic burden or joy...depending on how you look at it...squarely on the shoulders of your student-athlete to be sure to earn an acceptable grade point average that is achievable. In fact, it can all be achieved when you know in advance what is expected. The biggest challenge is time. There is just *not* enough time to recover from an *unacceptable* grade point average that takes all of high school to earn. It doesn't matter how well your student athlete performed on the ACT or SAT college entrance exams. If your student-athlete does *not* have an acceptable grade point average, then they may not be able to receive scholarship opportunities or participate in sports in some colleges or universities.

Sometimes, when talking to people that I know or even just met, I ask some of the following questions in the next section just to see how much is known about high school student-athletes and college scholarship opportunities.

**Did you know?**

- Over 7.6 million high school student-athletes participate in sports according to the National Federation of State High School Associations (NFHS).

- A high school student-athlete that dreams of participating in and receiving scholarships for sports at Division I or Division II level colleges or universities must first be certified by the NCAA Eligibility Center (National Collegiate Athletic Association) for acceptable academic classes and grades.

- The official certification is earned when your student-athlete successfully completes acceptable classes as determined by the NCAA Eligibility Center and must achieve a grade point average (GPA), ACT or SAT score that is met on a sliding scale also determined by the NCAA Eligibility Center.

- Student-athlete moms typically don't know how to guide their high school student-athlete through the NCAA Eligibility Center to receive an official certification to play college sports at the Division I and Division II levels. Some make the discovery in their student-athlete's senior year when it's too late to substantially improve their GPA that is a required component.

- There are other college scholarship opportunities available for your student-athlete.

- Community service and/or hobbies are questions on college applications.

If you knew *all* of the information above, then you may want to skip this chapter. If you're like I was and didn't know *any* of this information, then keep reading student-athlete mom. You'll be glad you did! I'm no longer amazed that student-athlete moms simply do not know this information. That is why I wrote this book so that student-athlete moms everywhere have the opportunity to learn this information before it's too late to help your child manage high school with sports and get college scholarship opportunities. So let's go a head and discuss each of the *Did you know?* items and later discover how the guidance department can help your student-athlete in these areas.

**Did you know?**

- **Over 7.6 million high school student-athletes participate in sports according to the National Federation of State High School Associations (NFHS).**

The National Federation of State High School Associations is also referred to as NFHS and was established in 1920. Its headquarters is located in Indianapolis, Indiana. There is an association representing high schools in each of the 50 states and the District of Columbia. For example: California Interscholastic Federation, Indiana High School Athletic Association, Virginia High School League, etc.

Student-athlete moms may want to check out their own state organization to learn the number of student-athletes that participate in sports in their area. Some states have more student-athletes than others. You can find this information by contacting the NFHS for a hard copy of their "NFHS Handbook" that they publish each year.

**Contact Information:**

National Federation of State High School Associations
690 W. Washington Street
Indianapolis, IN 46204

Phone:   (317) 972-6900
Fax:     (317) 822-5700
Website: www.nfhs.org

**Did you know?**

- **A high school student-athlete that dreams of participating in and receiving scholarships for sports at Division I or Division II level colleges or universities must first be certified by the NCAA (National Collegiate Athletic Association) Eligibility Center for acceptable academic classes and grades.**

The National Collegiate Athletic Association is also referred to as the NCAA and was established in 1906. It has an official NCAA Eligibility Center. Student-athletes must meet their guidelines to be able to receive scholarships to participate in sports at the Division I or Division II level. The NCAA Eligibility Center also provides guidelines for Division III level colleges and universities.

Sport scholarships that are available at the Division I and Division II levels may not be awarded to your student-athlete unless he or she is first certified by the NCAA Eligibility Center. The certification is for specific types of classes taken in high school, an acceptable grade point average (GPA), and an acceptable score on the ACT or SAT exams.

**Contact Information:**

National Collegiate Athletic Association
700 W. Washington Street
Indianapolis, IN 46204

Phone:   (317) 916-4255
Fax:      (317) 917-6222
Website: www.ncaa.org

The Internet website for the NCAA Eligibility Center provides information that will help your student-athlete and you with everything you need to know about becoming certified as follows.

www.eligibilitycenter.org

Search for:

NCAA College-Bound Student-Athlete
- or -
High School Administrators (guidance counselor)

There is additional information provided by the NCAA Eligibility Center that is extremely important. It's a guide that is very easy to read and will provide you with just about everything you need to know to help your student-athlete get certified by the NCAA Eligibility Center for taking the right type of classes in high school and earning acceptable grades. It's a lot easier than you may think. You just need to be sure to take the time to read the entire guide from cover to cover. This guide is updated each school year, so be sure to download the current version each high school year until your student-athlete enters college.

To get your **Guide for the College-Bound Student-Athlete**:

www.eligibilitycenter.org

Search for:

Guide for the College-Bound Student-Athlete

**Did you know?**

- **The official certification is earned when your student-athlete successfully completes acceptable classes as determined by the NCAA Eligibility Center and must achieve a grade point average (GPA), ACT or SAT score that is met on a sliding scale also determined by the NCAA Eligibility Center.**

The NCAA Eligibility Center information in the previous section provides the list of classes already approved for your student-athlete to take at his or her high school. On the NCAA Eligibility Center website, there is a link for most high schools that lists the specific classes. This makes it very easy for your student-athlete, Guidance Counselor, and you to be sure all requirements have been met.

In the previous section, there was information about how to get your **Guide for the College-Bound Student Athlete**. This is where you will find the requirements for the grade point average (GPA), ACT, and SAT scores.

You will learn that the higher the grade point average, the lower your student-athlete can score on either the ACT or SAT. The higher the ACT or SAT score, then a lower grade point average is acceptable by the NCAA Eligibility Center. This process is what I refer to as a *sliding scale*.

Some student-athletes perform very well in the classroom but are *not* good standardized test takers like the ACT or SAT. So the sliding scale will be to their advantage when getting test results.

Other student-athletes do *not* perform well in the classroom but are very good standardized test takers like the ACT or SAT. So the sliding scale will also be to their advantage when getting test results.

**LOVING MOM WARNING!!!** The minimum ACT or SAT score required by the National Collegiate Athletic Association (NCAA) may be different from the minimum score required by the college or university of interest to your student-athlete. I highly recommend that you contact the Admissions Department at the college or university to learn what their minimum score requirements are for both the ACT and SAT. This information will help you in conversations with the high school Guidance Department and the Admissions Department plus the coach at the potential college or university.

**Did you know?**

- **Student-athlete moms typically don't know how to guide their high school student-athlete through the NCAA Eligibility Center to receive an official certification to play college sports at the Division I and Division II levels. Some make the discovery in their student-athlete's senior year when it is too late to substantially improve their GPA that is a required component.**

There is a lot of scholarship information out there for student-athletes. I've just not found any that's designed especially for moms. That's another reason why I was inspired to write this book. Student-athlete moms spend the most time with their child during high school years and have the ability to influence them to pursue college scholarships. Unless the mom was a former student-athlete, she may not understand how to help her child manage high school with sports and get college scholarship opportunities.

**Did you know?**

- **There are other college scholarships available for your student-athlete.**

Oh yes there are!

Your student-athlete does *not* have to attend a Division I or Division II school governed by the National Collegiate Athletic Association (NCAA) where they may participate in sports.

In addition, your child may *still* attend a Division I or Division II school governed by the NCAA for its education and *not* play sports.

There are also very good colleges and universities affiliated with the NCAA at the Division III level where your student-athlete may play sports. However, I believe your child cannot accept any *sports* scholarships at those schools. Contact those colleges and universities directly to discover what other eligible scholarships are available for your student-athlete.

Finally, there are many private colleges and universities that accept all kinds of student-athletes for the love of education and offer wonderful scholarships. So don't hesitate to also explore those college scholarship opportunities!

**LOVING MOM WARNING!!!** You just may find an amazing school that is a good fit for your child because of the *life skills* we learned about in the Athletic Department chapter that have nothing to do with physically participating in a sports. Remember the chapter on the Athletic Department and the 20 life skills? Yes, isn't life great! And all the hard work as a student-athlete may pay off one way or another.

**Did you know?**

- **Community service and/or hobbies are questions on college applications?**

If your student-athlete is already involved in community service, then this question will be answered easily.

If your student-athlete has *not* been involved in community service, they will want to find some volunteer opportunity that they are passionate about and start serving today! They will then be able to answer this question on the application in a *credible* manner.

There are plenty of volunteer organizations to contact in your area. A few categories are listed below.

Local religious organizations

Local hospitals

Other organizations can be discovered at www.unitedway.org

Other organizations can be discovered at www.serve.gov

You may be wondering what does the guidance department have to do with everything in the previous sections of this chapter. Well let me share with you exactly *how* and *why* the guidance department is a valuable resource to your student-athlete in everything you've learned in this chapter.

Let's start with student-athlete moms need to know who is leading the guidance department and that includes the Administrative Assistant who can help you when others are not available. Take a moment to write down their information below and keep it updated.

**Guidance Department Director**

_____ name

_____ phone

_____ email

## Assistant Guidance Department Director

_____ name

_____ phone

_____ email

## Administrative Assistant
## Receptionist

_____ name

_____ phone

_____ email

Some schools have a counselor whose primary purpose is to help your child with *college* information for planning purposes. Take a moment to write down their information below and keep it updated.

**College Counselor**

_____ name

_____ phone

_____ email

Some schools have a counselor whose primary purpose is to help your child with *career* information to help with college planning. Take a moment to write down their information below and keep it updated.

**Career Counselor**

_____ name

_____ phone

_____ email

Don't be surprised if the same person at the school provides both college and career counseling. It's also important to know which counselor will help your child during each of the four high school years of $9^{th}$ grade freshman, $10^{th}$ grade sophomore, $11^{th}$ grade junior, and $12^{th}$ grade senior. Sometimes, counselors are assigned to a particular grade or year in school. Take a moment to write down their information and keep it updated.

**Guidance Counselor**
**$9^{th}$ Grade – Freshman Year**

_____ name

_____ phone

_____ email

## Guidance Counselor
### 10th Grade – Sophomore Year

_____ name

_____ phone

_____ email

## Guidance Counselor
### 11th Grade – Junior Year

_____ name

_____ phone

_____ email

**Guidance Counselor**
**12th Grade – Senior Year**

_____ name

_____ phone

_____ email

## Guidance Department Like a Shadow

The guidance department is like a *shadow* to your student-athlete when it comes to becoming certified by the NCAA Eligibility Center. They are the *academic* point of contact for your student-athlete. The guidance department is required to help complete a special form with information about the successful completion of your student-athlete's courses and grades that make up the point average (GPA) and sends it directly to the NCAA. Earlier in this chapter, I provided you the following NCAA Eligibility Center information for both your student-athlete and Guidance Counselor.

www.eligibilitycenter.org

*Search for:*

NCAA College-Bound Student-Athlete
- or -
High School Administrators (guidance counselor)

If your student-athlete's Guidance Counselor doesn't already know about this website, please be a *parent partner* and share this information. I know that the NCAA and NFHS associations do a very good job of making sure Guidance Counselors at high schools have this information. However, in the event yours doesn't, you can now share! The important thing to remember is that a student-athlete should *not* just send in a report card to the NCAA to be certified.

If you haven't figured it out already, to be certified by the NCAA Eligibility Center is totally based on *academics*. Grades matter! The ACT with an acceptable score matters! The SAT with an acceptable score matters! I think you get the point. I will discuss the ACT and SAT later on in this chapter. However, let's stay focused on getting certified right now. Your student-athlete may earn the right to be certified by the NCAA Eligibility Center by taking classes with acceptable grades and taking the ACT and/or the SAT with acceptable scores. Remember that not every guidance department knows the detailed process for your student-athlete to become certified by the NCAA Eligibility Center. That's where you come in to "save the day" as student-athlete mom as *parent partner*! The information you learn in this book will help you share information with the Guidance Counselor that they may not know. Of course it will be up to the Guidance Counselor to personally take care of their responsibilities as determined by the NCAA. But it doesn't hurt at all for you to support them with information you can provide.

## Academic Performance Can *Make or Break* Your Student-Athlete

Some of the best student-athletes do not always perform equally as good in the classroom and cannot be certified by the NCAA Eligibility Center. I know it's hard to believe, but it's true. These type of situations open up opportunities for less than the best physically talented student-athletes to get college scholarship opportunities. Let's face it; colleges have already invested in the sport of interest for your student-athlete. That means they have set aside scholarship monies to recruit student-athletes. In fact, they work extremely hard all year recruiting what they believe is the best possible talent for their college or university. In a perfect world, they get their student-athletes for the current year and move onto recruiting for the next year. However, there are a few specific challenges that college recruiters may face as follows.

- The student-athlete does not take acceptable classes as determined by the NCAA.

- The student-athlete does not achieve the minimum GPA as determined by the NCAA.

- The student-athlete does not achieve the minimum ACT score as determined by the NCAA.

- The student-athlete does not achieve the minimum SAT score as determined by the NCAA.

- The guidance department and/or principal do not send in the required forms to the NCAA.

- The student-athlete does not register for an NCAA Eligibility Certification.

## Take Acceptable Classes

The summer *before* your student-athlete enters high school as a freshman is a great time to meet with the Guidance Counselor to discuss and plan acceptable classes as determined by the NCAA. Some may think this is too premature. However, you don't want your student-athlete to get too far along in high school only to discover you're missing an acceptable class or two. The good news is that most high schools already have acceptable classes as part of their regular course schedule. Just to be sure, share the following NCAA Eligibility Center website information below with the Guidance Counselor.

www.eligibilitycenter.org

*Search for:*

NCAA College-Bound Student-Athlete
- or -
High School Administrators (guidance counselor)

## Grade Point Average (GPA)

I once sat and listened to a panel of students, to hear some state that they really didn't know about the meaning of a GPA or take it seriously until they were well into high school. Ouch! Talk about digging an academic hole right away. Not a great way to start high school, but it happens every day. I heard it with my own ears!

One of the best ways to love all over your student-athlete child is to teach about the importance of the GPA at the *beginning* of their 8th grade year and *before* they start high school. Use their entire 8th grade year to *practice* what it means to have a GPA when it won't count towards high school. The fact of the matter is that on *day one* of high school every homework assignment, quiz, test, and sometimes attendance with participation points count towards their GPA. It adds up along the way to a final GPA when they graduate in four years from high school. There's no turning back the clock! More importantly, it's harder to try to *make-up* a GPA by getting better grades the rest of their high school career than being sure to *earn and keep* the highest grades possible from *day one* of freshman year.

I actually know a student-athlete that received an acceptable score on the ACT and SAT exams but did not earn an acceptable GPA as determined by the NCAA Eligibility Center sliding scale range.

Yes, you guessed it! The NCAA Eligibility Center could not certify the student-athlete to participate in sports at the Division I and Division II levels. Having learned all of this, can you afford *not* to stress the importance of the GPA to your student-athlete *before* they start high school? Remember, 8th grade is a great practice year. So use it!

Your student-athlete and you should build a relationship with the Guidance Counselor throughout high school to ensure any questions you may have about the GPA as it relates to the NCAA Eligibility Center gets answered immediately. You may be surprised that there is a slight difference in how your high school determines your student-athlete's GPA from how it is determined by the NCAA Eligibility Center. Visit your student-athlete's Guidance Counselor for an explanation of how the NCAA Eligibility Center does not factor in *all* of the classes taken by your student-athlete. Remember that earlier in this book we discussed the specific type of classes. If your student-athlete takes extra classes beyond the list provided by the NCAA Eligibility Center, those classes will *not* be factored in as part of the GPA determined by the NCAA Eligibility Center. However, your student-athlete's high school will factor those classes in as it determines appropriate. Once again, visiting your student-athlete's Guidance Counselor is a great way to be sure you get all the answers to your questions about GPA.

*Carefully review the course requirements for your student-athlete to be certified by the NCAA Eligibility Center using the information below.*

www.eligibilitycenter.org

*Search for:*

NCAA College-Bound Student-Athlete
- or -
High School Administrators (guidance counselor)

*Next, setup a meeting with your student-athlete's Guidance Counselor to review the course schedule for your student-athlete for 9th through 12th grade. I used this time to plan all four years of high school for my student-athlete so that I would not have to have a meeting each year. I then followed-up each year to be sure classes had not changed. The relationship I built with the Guidance Counselor enabled her to also contact me in advance of any class changes so that we could be sure my student-athlete met the NCAA Eligibility Center course requirements.*

*After discussing high school class options and the NCAA Eligibility Center with your student-athlete, go ahead and write the courses in the next section. Use this section to communicate with your student-athlete and Guidance Counselor throughout the high school experience. You'll be glad you did!*

## 9TH grade—Freshman Year

## 10th Grade—Sophomore Year

## 11th Grade—Junior Year

## 12th Grade—Senior Year

## ACT (American College Testing)

Have you ever wondered what ACT stands for? As a student-athlete mom, I wanted to know a little about this test. It's the American College Testing (ACT) that was established in the 1950s. The following website link provides you *history* about this college entrance exam.

http://www.act.org/aboutact/history.html

The following is their website link for registration, test preparation, fees, scores, college planning, financial aid, and even career planning.

http://www.actstudent.org

The website provides ACT test schedules for the entire school year. Make sure your student-athlete meets with the Guidance Counselor to help identify when and where to take the test and to learn about the registration process.

## SAT (Scholastic Achievement Test)

Have you also ever wondered what SAT stands for? It is the Scholastic Achievement Test. I could not locate its own website with its *history*. However, the following website link provides you history about this college entrance exam.

http://www.eduers.com/sat/history_of_sat.htm

The following is their website link for practice, registration, scores, and other information about the test.

http://sat.collegeboard.org/home

The website provides SAT test schedules for the entire school year. Make sure your student-athlete meets with the Guidance Counselor to help identify when and where to take the test and to learn about the registration process.

**Financial Aid**

Some student-athlete moms don't have to worry about paying for college, and we're genuinely happy for them. But there are a whole lot of us that do! Get use to the term *financial aid* when discussing college. It can mean any of the following.

- Athletic scholarships that do *not* have to be paid back.
- Academic scholarships that do *not* have to be paid back.
- Grants that do *not* have to be paid back.

- Federal student loans that *do* have to be paid back.
- Other student loans that *do* have to be paid back.
- Other parent loans that *do* have to be paid back.

Unless you're paying 100% *cash* for your student-athlete, financial aid will become a way of life in college! There is even an official Financial Aid Office in just about every college or university.

Before a college or university can determine how much scholarships, grants, or student loans your student-athlete may be eligible to receive, a **FREE Application for Federal Student Aid** must be completed on the Internet. If you do not have a computer at home, you will want to visit your student-athlete's Guidance Counselor or the local library to use its computer to complete the application that *requires* both parent and child information. The following is the website link with all of the information you need to complete the application.

http://www.fafsa.ed.gov/

**Love the Guidance Department**

Hopefully you can now understand why some of the very best athletically talented student-athletes may *not* be able to receive college scholarship opportunities at the Division I and Division II levels. If the student-athlete does not earn an acceptable grade point average (GPA) and ACT or SAT score, then they cannot be certified by the NCAA Eligibility Center. Although this creates college scholarship opportunities for other student-athletes, I find it sad that many student-athletes and their moms may not have known about all of the details in this book before entering high school when the outcome could have been more positive to be certified by the NCAA Eligibility Center.

Your student-athlete and you have a lot to discuss with the guidance department about receiving college scholarships that are academic based on grades, athletic based on sports, or both. Regardless of what type of scholarship, grades matter! The ACT with an acceptable score matters! The SAT with an acceptable score matters! I think you now understand the point. So what are you waiting for? Use the upcoming notes and personal plan in the next section to help your student-athlete.

**Notes ♥ Personal Plan**

# The Principal

**Official Leader**

This chapter is meant to be short but very important. This is a case where *less* is *more*. The Principal is the official point of contact as the *leader* of the school. Your student-athlete should get to know the Principal on good terms. Also, have contact information for the Principal in the event it is needed. Go ahead and take a moment to write down the important names and contact information for the Principal and his or her staff and keep it updated.

**Principal**

_____ name

_____ phone

_____ email

## Assistant Principal

_____ name

_____ phone

_____ email

## Administrative Assistant

_____ name

_____ phone

_____ email

In the next **Notes ♥ Personal Plan** section you may want to journal ways that your student-athlete can build some sort of relationship with the Principal. I have seen many Principals of high schools at sporting events and often wondered how well they know the student-athletes outside of sports. It is my hope that they make every effort to get to know *all* of the students in the high school they lead.

In the event a college or university recruiter contacts the Principal, he or she should personally know your student-athlete and be able to have a genuine conversation about the different areas of your child instead of just sports. Having the discussion about the importance of this relationship may help your student-athlete with confidence to build a relationship with the Principal.

**Notes ♥ Personal Plan**

# Your Student-Athlete

**Roles and Responsibilities**

Where does your student-athlete fit into all of the information discussed so far in this book? Everywhere! He or she has *everything* to gain! The more college scholarships, the less your family will pay in expenses. You'll be able to provide *other* things your student-athlete may *want* while away at college. Explain to your student-athlete that the ability to earn scholarships while in high school may leave extra money for the family to obtain things *wanted* while away in college. Otherwise the money will have to go to *needed* college expenses with little or nothing left for *wants*.

**Here's a general list of roles and responsibilities to discuss with your student-athlete.**

- Maintain a positive, optimistic attitude during good and challenging times.

- Focus on attending all classes and be on time.

- Concentrate on earning the best possible grades for a high GPA (grade point average).

- Enjoy the high GPA throughout high school and keep it that way!

- Build a genuine relationship with members of the guidance department.

- Perform at your *personal best* in your sport.

- Build a genuine relationship with members of the athletic department beyond the sport.

- Build a genuine relationship with the Principal and staff.

- Participate in all activities discussed in the next Student-Athlete Marketing chapter.

- Complete and return any college recruiting questionnaires immediately! Remember that the recruiter is interested in your child and probably 15 other student-athletes for the exact same position. The recruiter will eventually choose only one student-athlete for the position. So don't *give* them a reason *not* to choose you!

- Immediately follow-up with *all* colleges and universities of interest.

**Notes ♥ Personal Plan**

# Student-Athlete Marketing

**No Experience Necessary**

All of the chapters in this book that you have read up to this point should empower you to believe you have all of the *tools* necessary to market your student-athlete to colleges and universities. You *don't* need experience in student-athlete marketing. Remember the first time you gazed into the sweet little face of your bundle of joy. Remember your bonding moment of love and personal commitment that you would do anything for your child. Remember that nothing would separate you from exploring all possibilities to bring joy to your child every day of his or her life. Remember that no one could ever know your child as good as you, because you are his or her mom. You took great pride in being a mom then and still do today. This is all the *courage* and *strength* you need to help market your student-athlete to colleges and universities for scholarship opportunities. Plus I'm going to share with you what I did to help my student-athlete receive over $40,000 in college scholarships. It made the world of difference to our family budget. Thank God!

Think of this book as a *toolkit* and every piece of information you've learned is a *tool*. You now have lots of tools. After reading this book, student-athlete moms now have a *personal toolkit* and should not be afraid to use it! I don't care if you've never marketed anything in your life. I was in your same situation. If I could bump through it to gain $40,000 in college scholarships for my student-athlete, so can you! As you proceed, please always remember that your student-athlete is only looking to accept *one* college or university and its scholarship offer. Your student-athlete may be talented, but I believe he or she can attend and participate in sports at only *one* college or university at a time!

**Marketing Resources**

There are a lot of student-athlete marketing resources out there. Feel free to find one that you believe will help your student-athlete receive college scholarship opportunities. However, I will be providing a great tip on one that was given to me by my family. You may recall that I didn't learn about the information in this book until Thanksgiving holiday of my student-athlete's senior year of high school when he had finished his final football season. One of the resources my family gave me was the following book that I found very easy to read and provided all of the information I used to market and help my student-athlete get the $40,000 in college scholarships.

>Author:   Dion Wheeler

>Title:   A parent's and student-athlete's guide to athlete scholarships: Getting money without being taken for a (Full) ride

**LOVING MOM WARNING!!!** I highly encourage each student-athlete mom to purchase this book right away to get started reading sooner than later so that you can help your student athlete get college scholarship opportunities. The way I see it, the $40,000 that my student-athlete received in college scholarships far outweighs the price my family paid for Wheeler's book.

Dion Wheeler's book taught me many things that are not covered in my book you are now reading. Wheeler owned a professional recruiting service and was a head coach at a university. He was also the parent of student-athletes. It is from this experience that Wheeler details the overall recruiting process. His book is a must read! The neat thing is that Wheeler wrote the first 84 pages filled with college recruiting information. Wheeler then took it one step further and used the remainder of the book as his wonderful catalog list for every college or university in the United States that offers sports and lists the specific sports for both men and women. Everything in one book! The following is the information that he provides on colleges and universities.

>State
>College or University Name
>Address
>Phone Number
>List of men's sports offered.
>List of women's sports offered.

I want to share even more with you and have focused my thoughts on Wheeler's particular chapters on *Constructing the Profile, The Cover Letter, The Videotape, Sending Credentials,* and *The Visit.*

**Constructing the Profile**

Wheeler provides a format and detailed information needed to prepare a *Profile* for your student-athlete. A Profile is like a personal resume of your student-athlete's accomplishments. I had no idea this even existed! It includes information to contact your student-athlete and high school plus other personal information. NCAA Eligibility Center information is included as well as FAFSA (FREE Application for Federal Student Aid). It also includes academic accomplishments. You'll be thrilled to recall that we already covered this information in the earlier Guidance Counselor chapter in this book.

Finally, Wheeler includes athletic information like coaches contact information and sports statistics that you can obtain from the athletic department for your child's particular sport. Isn't it exciting to know you can review the Athletic Department chapter in this book to get the contact information? However, you will have to contact them directly to provide you the sports statistics that they keep for your student-athlete. Wheeler provides in his book examples of statistics by sport so that you'll know what to request from the athletic department. They may even provide you more statistics. Politely take it and include it in the profile. Are you feeling empowered yet?

**The Cover Letter**

I couldn't believe that not only did Wheeler give advice on what should be included in a cover letter, he provided a wonderful sample! Your student-athlete can simply personalize it with his or her own information. Priceless!

**The Videotape**

This was an area that I was very glad Wheeler included in his book. Of course you can replace the word videotape with DVD or any technology format you choose. I admit that I saw cameras at my student-athletes games but never thought about ever needing to request the video for use. Most high schools video their athletic events and keep it on file in the athletic department or even the library. They are typically very willing to provide you with the video. So you know where to start to request video for your student-athlete.

Wheeler carefully explained what should be included in a video that includes it length. Once again, Wheeler does a very good job providing detailed information and examples that makes it very easy.

**Sending Credentials**

What colleges or universities should receive your student-athlete's marketing information? What coaches should it be addressed to? Will your student-athlete *really* want to attend that college or university? How many colleges and universities should receive the information? Wheeler explores each of these questions so that your student-athlete can make very good, informed decisions.

**The Visit**

The college visit is my final section of focus on Wheeler's book. Recruiters may invite your student-athlete to visit their college or university. Or your student-athlete may choose to visit a particular college or university on his or her own. Wheeler discusses what offices to visit, provides tips, and even a list of questions to ask during the visit in the areas of athletic, academic, legal, and financial.

**Proceed with extreme caution!!!**

Check with your student-athlete's Guidance Counselor about how excused absences are permitted for college visits and during what year in high school. Keep in mind that missing high school for college visits is a privilege and *not* a right.

Next, verify with the NCAA (National Collegiate Athletic Association) about when visits are permitted. You will also want to verify how many visits are permitted in a given school year. In addition, the NCAA has college guidelines on any type of contact with student-athletes whether it's by mail, email, phone, or in person. You want to *be sure* your student-athlete does *not* get disqualified for college scholarships in sports based on breaking *any* rules.

The easiest way to get information is to get a copy of the **Guide for the College-Bound Student-Athlete** that we learned about in the previous Guidance Department chapter.

To get your **Guide for the College-Bound Student-Athlete**:

www.eligibilitycenter.org

*Search for:*

Guide for the College-Bound Student-Athlete

**The Questionnaire**

Recruiters that are interested in your student-athlete may send an initial questionnaire. **Complete and return it immediately!** The recruiter is interested in your child and probably 15 other student-athletes for the exact same position. I thought it might be fun to share with you information requested on a Questionnaire that my student-athlete received from a university.

**PERSONAL INFORMATION**
- Name
- Nickname
- Address
- City
- State
- Birth Date
- Year of Graduation
- Social Security Number
- E-mail
- Home Phone
- Cell Phone
- Other Phone
- Father
- Occupation
- Mother
- Occupation
- Live With
- Siblings/Ages
- Hobbies

**ATHLETIC INFORMATION**
- Height
- Weight
- Jersey Number
- Position
- Years Played in High School
- Points/Game
- Assists/Game
- Rebounds/Game
- Steals/Game
- High School Coach
- Home Phone
- Work Phone
- Cell Phone
- AAU Team
- AAU Coach
- Home Phone
- Work Phone
- Cell Phone
- Athletic Achievement/Honors
- List Your Top Three College Choices

**ACADEMIC INFORMATION**
- High School
- City
- State
- School Phone
- Guidance Counselor
- Phone
- GPA
- PSAT Score
- SAT Score & Date Taken
- ACT Score & Date Taken

**MISCELLANEOUS**
- Registered with the NCAA Eligibility Center?
- College/Major Interest
- Academic Achievement/Honors
- Relatives or Friends Who Attended University
- Who Will Help You Make Your College Choice?

## When Should I Start Marketing?

This is an excellent question! We must keep in mind that our child will go through *four* years of high school maturing and learning in academics and athletics. However, *day one* of *freshman year* begins gathering marketing information. This doesn't mean you have to send it to a college or university. It just means that keeping your student-athlete on track to maintain as high a GPA (grade point average) as possible, doing his or her personal best on the ACT and/or SAT college entrance exam and in their sport will go a long way in making life much easier when preparing to market your child.

Once I had learned so much from my first student-athlete, I was able to use the following plan to help my second student-athlete manage high school with sports and get college scholarship opportunities. The following is helpful advice and guidance for your student-athlete.

### 9th Grade—Freshman Year

- Focus on attending all classes and on time.

- Concentrate on earning the best grades possible for a high GPA (grade point average).

### 10th Grade—Sophomore Year

- Start to enjoy the GPA and keep it that way!

- Register with the NCAA Eligibility Center before the school year ends, because the beginning of 11th grade is when college recruiters become even more active. You'll want to have the registration behind you when your student-athlete begins 11th grade.

- Request the Guidance Counselor send in the required information to the NCAA Eligibility Center immediately following your student-athletes registration.

### 11th Grade—Junior Year

- In the fall and as soon as your student-athlete returns to high school, send marketing materials to all colleges and universities that your student-athlete is interested in attending.

- Complete and return any recruiting questionnaires immediately! Remember that the college recruiter is interested in your child and probably 15 other student-athletes for the same position.

- Request the Guidance Counselor update required information to the NCAA Eligibility Center at the end of the school year.

### 12th Grade—Senior Year

- Follow-up with colleges and universities of interest.

- Make college visits sooner than later in the year.

- Request the Guidance Counselor finalize required information to the NCAA Eligibility Center immediately following your student-athletes final grades.

**Today's Technology**

My final thought about marketing your student-athlete is to explore the use of technology that is available today. I can remember us typing a hard copy letter to go with videotape, making labels to put on envelopes, sealing it, and driving to the Post Office to mail off the marketing package. I can also remember the phone as the only use of follow-up communication. Today, communication is much more effective and easier with technology through the use of texting, email, and other uses of the Internet. Discover what works best for your student-athlete, you, and the colleges and universities.

**Notes ♥ Personal Plan**

# Good Luck With That

**For the Love of Your Child**

You are a mom that provides *unconditional love* and *support* for your child. You've now explored many possibilities to continue to bring joy to your student-athlete. You're an amazing student-athlete mom! The final chapter is what I fondly refer to as "Get luck with that!" It was my loving way of saying to my student-athlete children that they were at their *personal best* when trying to achieve a goal whether it be getting a better grade in a class, performing well on a quiz or test, or breaking a school record in their sport.

I *strongly* encourage each of you to believe you have been empowered through what you've learned in this book to help your student-athlete manage high school with sports and get college scholarship opportunities. Always remember that the scholarships may be academic based on grades, athletic based on sport, or both!

When your student-athlete receives scholarships to participate in sports, you will know that you helped him or her manage high school with sports and get the college scholarship opportunities. On the other hand, if after all we've discussed in this book and you took action to market your child, your student-athlete does not participate in sports or get scholarships, refer back to the chapter on the Athletic Department that outlined the 20 *life skills* that were learned through the world of sports. It was hardly a waste of time for your student-athlete to participate in sports! These transferable skills from sports may be the best preparation your student-athlete ever has to be prepared for college and life in general. Remember, it was about being your child's biggest fan on the journey to a wonderful college education through the world of sports. Sports attributed to your child receiving the opportunity to be a loved, productive citizen of society through education. What more can a mom want?

## Sports Inspire

People are first *inspired within* to be *motivated to act* in a certain behavior. The high school inspiration to participate in college sports can motivate your student-athlete to be at his or her personal best at achieving a very good GPA (grade point average) to be accepted to a college or university.

## Education Matters

A college education increases the chance that your child will have a higher income level as an adult to help provide for his or her family. This means your grandchildren may have an even better life. Isn't that what this world is suppose to be about? Preparing the way for an even better life each generation.

## Make a Positive, Meaningful Difference in the World

Sports and education...what a wonderful combination! Thank you in advance for reading this book sooner than later and sharing what you've learned with every mom you know. Remember that sharing information empowers each of us to make a positive, meaningful difference in this world. Be empowered now!

## Your Personal Plan

We're almost finished. But first, the final section of this book is dedicated to you developing a *Student-Athlete Mom Empowerment Plan* with ten action steps. Based on what you learned in this book, write down ten action steps you are committed to take to help your student-athlete manage high school with sports and get college scholarship opportunities. For the love of your student-athlete, take action to develop your plan now!

## Student-Athlete Mom Empowerment Plan
♥ ♥ ♥ ♥
## Action No. 1

*Who* is involved?

_____

_____


*What* do I need to do?

_____

_____


*Why* do I need to do it?

_____

_____

*Where* do I need to get it accomplished?

―――――――――――――――――――――――

―――――――――――――――――――――――

*How* will I get it accomplished?

―――――――――――――――――――――――

―――――――――――――――――――――――

## Student-Athlete Mom Empowerment Plan
♥ ♥ ♥ ♥
### Action No. 2

*Who* is involved?

_____

_____


*What* do I need to do?

_____

_____


*Why* do I need to do it?

_____

_____

*Where* do I need to get it accomplished?

_____

_____


*How* will I get it accomplished?

_____

_____

## Student-Athlete Mom Empowerment Plan
♥ ♥ ♥ ♥
## Action No. 3

*Who* is involved?

---
---

*What* do I need to do?

---
---

*Why* do I need to do it?

---
---

*Where* do I need to get it accomplished?

_____

_____


*How* will I get it accomplished?

_____

_____

## Student-Athlete Mom Empowerment Plan
♥ ♥ ♥ ♥
### Action No. 4

*Who* is involved?

 

---

---

*What* do I need to do?

 

---

---

*Why* do I need to do it?

 

---

---

*Where* do I need to get it accomplished?

_____

_____


*How* will I get it accomplished?

_____

_____

## Student-Athlete Mom Empowerment Plan
♥ ♥ ♥ ♥
## Action No. 5

*Who* is involved?

_____

_____


*What* do I need to do?

_____

_____


*Why* do I need to do it?

_____

_____

*Where* do I need to get it accomplished?

_____

_____


*How* will I get it accomplished?

_____

_____

## Student-Athlete Mom Empowerment Plan
♥ ♥ ♥ ♥
### Action No. 6

*Who* is involved?

_____

_____


*What* do I need to do?

_____

_____


*Why* do I need to do it?

_____

_____

*Where* do I need to get it accomplished?

_____

_____

*How* will I get it accomplished?

_____

_____

## Student-Athlete Mom Empowerment Plan

♥ ♥ ♥ ♥

### Action No. 7

*Who* is involved?

_____

_____

*What* do I need to do?

_____

_____

*Why* do I need to do it?

_____

_____

*Where* do I need to get it accomplished?

_____

_____


*How* will I get it accomplished?

_____

_____

## Student-Athlete Mom Empowerment Plan
♥ ♥ ♥ ♥
## Action No. 8

*Who* is involved?

_____

_____


*What* do I need to do?

_____

_____


*Why* do I need to do it?

_____

_____

*Where* do I need to get it accomplished?

_____

_____


*How* will I get it accomplished?

_____

_____

## Student-Athlete Mom Empowerment Plan
♥ ♥ ♥ ♥
## Action No. 9

*Who* is involved?

_____

_____

*What* do I need to do?

_____

_____

*Why* do I need to do it?

_____

_____

*Where* do I need to get it accomplished?

_____

_____


*How* will I get it accomplished?

_____

_____

## Student-Athlete Mom Empowerment Plan

♥ ♥ ♥ ♥

## Action No. 10

*Who* is involved?

_____

_____

*What* do I need to do?

_____

_____

*Why* do I need to do it?

_____

_____

*Where* do I need to get it accomplished?

_____

_____


*How* will I get it accomplished?

_____

_____

www.ingramcontent.com/pod-product-compliance
Lightning Source LLC
Chambersburg PA
CBHW071701040426
42446CB00011B/1856